# The Philosophy of
# NUMBERS

**THEIR TONE AND COLORS**

VOLUME I

A SMALL GEM
BY
## MRS. L. DOW BALLIETT

# Some Other Titles From New Falcon Publications

*Aha! The Sevenfold Mystery of the Ineffable Love* —Aleister Crowley
*Aleister Crowley and the Treasure House of Images*
—J.F.C. Fuller, Aleister Crowley, Lon Milo DuQuette and Nancy Wasserman
*Aleister Crowley's Illustrated Goetia, Sex Magic, Tantra & Tarot:*
*An Insider's Guide to Robert Anton Wilson* —Eric Wagner
*Ask Baba Lon* —Lon Milo DuQuette
*Bio-Etheric Healing* —Trudy Lanitis
*Diary of the Antichrist* —David Cheribum
*Enochian Sex Magic and How To Workbook*
 —Aleister Crowley, Lon Milo DuQuette and Christopher S. Hyatt, Ph.D.
*Enochian World of Aleister Crowley* —DuQuette and Aleister Crowley
*Info-Psychology, Neuropolitique, The Game of Life, What Does WoMan Want?*
 —Timothy Leary, Ph.D.
*Nonlocal Nature: The Eight Circuits of Consciousness* —James A. Heffernan
*on What is* —Ja Wallin
*Pacts With The Devil, Urban Voodoo: A Beginner's Guide to Afro-Caribbean Magic*
 —Jason Black and Christopher S. Hyatt, Ph.D.
*Rebellion, Revolution and Religiousness* —Osho
*Rebels & Devils; The Psychology of Liberation*–Edited by **Christopher S. Hyatt, Ph.D.**
*Reichian Therapy: A Practical Guide for Home Use* —Dr. Jack Willis
*Shaping Formless Fire, Seizing Power, Taking Power*
*Secrets of Western Tantra: The Sexuality of the Middle Path*
*Dogma Daze* —Christopher S. Hyatt, Ph.D.
*Steamo Goes to Havana, The Social Epidemic of Child Abuse*
 —Michael Miller, M.Ed., M.S., Ph.D.
*The Illuminati Conspiracy: The Sapiens System* —Donald Holmes, M.D.
*The Magick In The Music and Other Essays* —Stephen Mace
*The Psychopath's Bible* —**Christopher S. Hyatt, Ph.D.**, and Jack Willis
*The Secret Inner Order Rituals of the Golden Dawn* —Pat Zalewski
*The Way of the Secret Lover Taboo: Sex, Religion & Magick*
 —C. Hyatt, Ph.D., and Lon DuQuette
*The Why, Who, and What of Existence* —Vlad Korbel
*Undoing Yourself With Energized Meditation and Other Devices*
*Woman's Orgasm: A Guide to Sexual Satisfaction*
 —Benjamin Graber M.D., and Georgia Kline-Graber, R.N.

## Other Titles by J. Marvin Spiegelman, Ph.D.

*A Modern Jew in Search of Soul*
*Buddhism and Jungian Psychology*
*Catholicism and Jungian Psychology*
*Hinduism and Jungian Psychology*
*Mysticism, Psychology and Oedipus - A Small Gem*
*Protestanism and Jungian Psychology*
*Psychotherapy and Religion at the Millennium and Beyond*
*Psychotherapy as a Mutual Process*
*Reich, Jung, Regardie & Me - The Unhealed Healer*
*Rider, Haggard, Henry Miller & I - The Unpublished Writer*
*Sufism, Islam and Jungian Psychology*
*The Knight - A Small Gem*
*The Nymphomaniac*
*The Quest - Further Adventures in the Unconscious*
*The Tree of Life - Paths in Jungian Individuation*
*The Wisdom of J. Marvin Speigelman Vol. I - Selected Writings*
*The Wisdom of J. Marvin Speigelman Vol. II - Psychology and Religion*

## Other Titles by Dr. Israel Regardie

*A Garden of Pomegranates*
*A Practical Guide to Geomantic Divination - A Small Gem*
*Attract and Use Healing Energy - A Small Gem*
*Be Yourself - A Guide to Relaxation and Health*
*Ceremonial Magic*
*Dr. Israel Regardie's Definitive Work on Aleister Crowley,*
  *The Eye In The Triangle*
*Healing Energy, Prayer and Relaxation*
*How To Make and Use Talismans - A Small Gem*
*Israel Regardie's The Foundations of Practical Magick*
*My Rosicrucian Adventure*
*Mysticism, Psychology and Oedipus - A Small Gem*
*Practical Magick - A Small Gem*
*Teachers of Fulfillment*
*The Art and Meaning of Magic - A Small Gem*
*The Body-Mind Connection, A Path to Well-Being - A Small Gem*
*The Complete Golden Dawn System of Magic*
*The Complete Golden Dawn System of Magic Book 1 - Ltd. Edition*
*The Complete Golden Dawn System of Magic Book 2 - Ltd. Edition*
*The Complete Golden Dawn System of Magic - The Black Edition*
*The Eye in the Triangle: An Interpretation of Aleister Crowley*
*The Golden Dawn Audio CDs, Vol. 1, Vol. 2, and Vol. 3*
*The Legend of Aleister Crowley*
*The Magic of Israel Regardie*
*The Middle Pillar*
*The Philosopher's Stone*
*The Portable Complete Golden Dawn System of Magic*
*The Tree of Life*
*The Wisdom of Israel Regardie - Vol. I*
  *Selected Introductions, Prefaces and Forewords*
*The Wisdom of Israel Regardie - Vol. II*
  *Selected Essays and Commentaries*
*The Wisdom of Israel Regardie - Vol. III*
  *Selected Articles, Introductions, Prefaces and Forewords*
*What You Should Know About the Golden Dawn*
*Wilhelm Reich, His Theory And Techniques*
*Aha!* (Dr. Israel Regardie and Aleister Crowley)
*Roll Away The Stone/The Herb Dangerous*
  (Dr. Israel Regardie and Aleister Crowley)

**MANY OF OUR TITLES AVAILABLE ON KINDLE!**
Please visit our website at http://www.newfalcon.com

Copyright © 2023 New Falcon Publications

All rights reserved. No part of this book,
in part or in whole, may be reproduced, transmitted,
or utilized, in any form or by any means, electronic or mechanical,
including photocopying, recording, or by any information storage
and retrieval system, without permission in writing
from the publisher, except for brief quotations
in critical articles, books and reviews.

ISBN 13: 978-156184-252-0
ISBN 10: 1-56184-252-4

New Falcon Publications First Edition 2023

The paper used in this publication meets the minimum requirements
of the American National Standard for Permanence of
Paper for Printed Library Materials Z39.48-1984

Printed in USA

NEW FALCON PUBLICATIONS
2046 Hillhurst Avenue
Los Angeles, California 90027
www.newfalcon.com
email: info@newfalcon.com

# The Philosophy of
# NUMBERS

### THEIR TONE AND COLORS

### VOLUME I

### A SMALL GEM
### BY
## MRS. L. DOW BALLIETT

NEW FALCON PUBLICATIONS
Los Angeles, California U.S.A.

# VOLUME I

## Contents

| CHAPTER | PAGE |
|---|---|
| Preface | 1 |
| 1. Your First Birth | 3 |
| 2. Eventful Births | 9 |
| 3. If We Have Individual Colors, When and How Did We First Receive Them? | 15 |
| 4. The Use of Birth Vibration | 19 |
| 5. The Meaning of Colors Disclosed Through Vibration of Numbers as Taught by Pythagoras | 23 |
| 6. Exercises to Develop Your Own Vibration or Birth Digit–The First Trinity | 29 |
| 7. Exercises–Continued–Free Numbers | 39 |
| 8. Your Name–Its Color and Sound | 43 |
| 9. Reading Individual Name Vibrations–The First Trinity | |
| 10. Reading Individual Name Numbers–4, 5, 6, 7 | 55 |
| 11. Free Numbers–8, 9, 11, 22 | 67 |

## MRS. L. DOW BALLIETT

A MASTER OF VIBRATIONS AND NUMEROLOGY, FOUNDER OF THE MASTER NUMBER SYSTEM, WHEREBY THE NUMBERS 11 AND 22 ARE NOT REDUCED. MRS. BALLIETT COMBINED PYTHAGORAS' WORK WITH BIBLICAL REFERENCE.

HER STUDENT, JUNO JORDAN, HELPED NUMEROLOGY BECOME THE SYSTEM KNOWN TODAY AS PYTHAGOREAN. MANY NUMEROLOGISTS TODAY STILL BASE THEIR WORK IN REFERENCE TO THESE WOMEN OF THE CALIFORNIA INSTITUTE OF NUMERICAL RESEARCH.

*This book is lovingly dedicated*
*to my niece*
**CAROLINA D. W. STILES**
*My life companion in search of truth and*
*my assistant in giving it expression.*
–The Author

# Preface

This book has been written in response to the requests of those who are interested in the study of Number Vibration. They came from all parts of the world asking for more of the simplified knowledge founded upon the one principal of Unity–that all things have but one source–and express in different forms the unity of the whole. The hidden strength or weakness of names, states, etc., as shown by the vowels have been evolved through the philosophy of numbers. From this source many unwritten laws can be made plain.

With greetings,<br>
The Author.

## CHAPTER 1

## Your First Birth

Whoever realizes himself as an individual part of this great universe, moved from cradle to grave by seen and unseen forces, no doubt has pondered upon at least two vital questions,–Why am I here? Why must I fill a place in life which appears so crowded with mistakes?

You know there must be a first cause for the individuality you are expressing. You know you are a soul in a body walking the earth and holding communication with like beings of limited memories.

The Bible teaches us that at the end of the seventh period Creation ceased. If this is true, where have you been during this long dim past between Creation's dawn and the present time? The place is of minor importance in comparison with what you have been doing since God sent out your soul as a ray of the Divine, holding within its vibration the ideal of becoming a perfect character.

In the course of ages Christ came to show us what a perfect character should be, and every conscious atom holds in latency the desire to become perfect. To reach this state of perfection it is necessary to battle sturdily with the earth currents to go through experiences of all kinds, until the man becomes a perfectly rounded and developed individual.

It is of little importance what kind of bodies your soul formed for itself when crossing the different spans of life, for its desire was always to grow into a perfect whole; which means a perfect embodiment, a perfect soul, and when perfect, the Spirit acknowledges it as being one with God.

Earth life may be likened to a child who is sent to a store for a loaf of bread, sugar and flour. He comes back bringing the bread but having forgotten the flour and sugar. He must return again and again to some state until he completes his whole errand successfully.

Some souls are laggards and are slow in doing the work their higher part chose for them, when they were freed from earth's dust. At this time they knew with the sure knowledge of the Spirit. As the ideal within the soul is always to grow into a perfect character, the place was chosen on the physical plane best suited to advance the soul in the lessons most needed.

When the individual, after coming to earth, yields to the lower earth currents and is not living at his highest, a constant and pervading feeling of unrest is ever present with him, until at last turning within, he finds in his higher self the true source of peace and happiness. When the higher self is recognized all the harmonies emerge. This self holds all the secrets of the past, the present and the future. When we live as we will some time live, when we know the physical and the spiritual law as one, then will we cease to grope blindly, for our path will be illumined from the light within.

When the conscious soul decides upon an earth life, with the eye of the Spirit it chooses that vibration in which to cross the span of life which holds the experiences it wishes to meet and overcome. The Divine stores the strength of its victories in its soul forces, and these we term strength of character or soul growth. Only those acts which have in some way benefitted humanity will find a place in the vibration of the soul, for it will accept only the good and true. Thus a human life may appear to be a failure and yet the soul will crown it for the growth it has made.

When a soul decides again to enter upon another work day of life in which to amend some weakness of character, it takes upon itself a mystical substance called the body with which to struggle with earth's vibrations. If in any incarnation the individual refuses to let the soul guide him, he makes but little progress, and like the child who did not do the errand well, he returns to his home having gained but little of that which he came to seek; not having made strong vibrations nor gained strength of character.

Unlike the body the soul will not masquerade and will express only the truth, so that when coming to this world it will be known by its own vibration which represents the moral strength it has earned in the past. It seeks parents and is born under natural law, holding positions in life from which it wishes to learn some needed lessons. Upon some one point the parent and child must vibrate together. This must be true of there would be no point of attraction between them. The child's soul seeks the soul love of the parent, the soul of the parent seeks the soul love of the child. There may be an antagonism upon the physical plane, but the higher self has called them together.

The most important point for the child is the time it comes to earth. As it comes of its own accord it chooses the place it needs either to gratify its ambition or to work in a limited sphere.

Your soul or higher self chose the position in life you are filling or should fill, and there is no vibration or number a soul can choose that is not sufficient for true happiness. Each vibration must be filled acceptably or you will return until you have successfully done your errand.

You selected your time of birth when certain constellations or planets were sending forth their own colors, so you selected your own colors through which to make the journey of life and were born in month, day and year in which the color you desired was in the atmosphere. The first objective breath you drew was filled with your own color and their force, and this color should surround you through life. When all its secrets have been revealed to you it will express itself in vibration of name, thus telling of a journey made in the past–a cycle earned. The child holds within its soul the knowledge of its past experiences and when a babe it has almost the same strength of soul as a grown man.

Not until the Trinity of Body, Soul and Spirit are attuned to earth life can the being fully realize what life holds. The more perfectly an embodiment is adjusted to the earth vibration, the more successfully can it do the work of its higher self.

When a name is to be given to a child it must vibrate to the exact soul growth attained. The soul will not masquerade. The intellect may desire to advance itself, but not until a growth is gained will the soul allow the statement to be made. Thousands of names bear almost the same vibration as a whole, yet have different forms such as John and Sarah, both of which vibrate to 2, yet one denotes a man and the other a woman, and the vowels are different. So a child's soul arises at the approach of baptism and silently influences its parents and guardians to a name expressing the vibration of the growth of its higher self. This accounts for the many changes of name even at the altar rail. The name shows the past growth of the individual and by carefully studying the number vibration you can catch glimpses of the struggles and victories of the past ages. By studying the birth number vibration of present life you can see what the individual wishes to gain in this incarnation. When he succeeds either consciously or unconsciously he will change his name in some way to show the strength of character gained in his life. Some have come to work to win; others to repair weak points, to do over work improperly done in the past.

If we believed the soul had its beginning in this present body we would have to believe in its end. We are one with the Divine, having lived always and will live forever. This theory explains many things otherwise inexplicable. One man rides in a rubber-tired coach with footmen sitting behind with folded arms, showing submission to his fellow man; another with black skin bears the burden of his race, while beside him walks one with the bearing and power of a king All these are but souls seeking growth in every phase of life, through every aspect of experience.

## CHAPTER 2
## Eventful Births

When the individual has successfully passed the limited vibrations–those under 8–and has entered the free vibrations (8, 9, 11, 22), his journeys through the events of earth are nearly an end. After this he usually comes as a helper to those who are bearing strong numbers. These people are far stronger than they appear. They are probably using only a part of their force, that part which is missionary. When we go to the South we take with us only light clothing. So men generally, as they walk the earth, appear very different from what they really are. Bodies are prone to masquerade, so we must look deeply into the soul to find of what the individual is capable and what he can overcome. By our own intellectual power we understand things in this world as great or small, but in the Spirit world there is no great neither is there small. So when men see great souls doing trifling work they sigh in pity and say "A wasted life." The pity is that they cannot understand. These great souls may be doing the necessary work to perfect the harmony of their vibration. You will find many advanced souls working a limited vibration shown in their birth number; some make mistakes, but try again and again to do that which is needful.

People who come to work and win usually have higher vibration of birth number than name number. This shows weakness in past growth, but the present active race, if won by the highest the individual knows, will gain for him strong free vibrations which will express themselves in name number.

In incarnating, a soul may seek a vibration that will draw to itself wealth; if this vibration is successfully met, in another life he may seek poverty, for in this way the soul learns its lessons. If in that environment of wealth it found the treasure it sought in a life of luxury, the memory of wealth clings to the soul; but if it was blinded by earth currents and was not a good guardian, it will always feel the pangs of poverty until it is strong enough to win that in which it failed in the past. After it has once succeeded, the fear of poverty is evermore removed; money and its rewards come in unexpected ways. Every victory won is stored up as character and shows in a strong vibration that is expressed to the world as a name. When a man shows a lack of strength, it does not mean the bearer can not win. This present life may be the starting point for a great victory. One may live at the highest of a weak vibration and win all it holds, and will contain enough to satisfy any one who does his best. Before this life is finished, his acts will make strong vibrations that will show in a changed named. No one will change or rearrange his name who has not earned a nigher new vibration. He will have no desire to do so. The soul is honest and will not deceive. The intellect may spasmodically try to do so, but the world will not recognize it, and the individual self will not hold it. But when it is once earned it will be recognized by the world and the individual holds to it as his own. We sometimes wonder why a man in bank and elsewhere signs his name John W. Smith when formerly he was known as J. Walker Smith. This man had outgrown his old environment and his higher self caused some circumstance to so affect him that he showed the strength of character he had gained by a changed name.

Pythagoras said the Heavens and Earth vibrate to the single numbers or digits of numbers. Each single number from 1 to 9 are digits.

To find you own numbers divide the alphabet into nine parts, thus:

| 1 | 2 | 3 | 4 | 5 | 6 | 7 | 8 | 9 |
|---|---|---|---|---|---|---|---|---|
| a | b | c | d | e | f | g | h | i |
| j | k | l | m | n | o | p | q | r |
| s | t | u | v | w | x | y | z | 9 |

Take for example the name Henry Elder.

**H** is found to vibrate to **8**
**E** is found to vibrate to **5**
**N** is found to vibrate to **5**
**R** is found to vibrate to **9**
**Y** is found to vibrate to **7**
$$\overline{34}$$

Add these numbers to find the digit of Henry, $\dfrac{\begin{array}{r}3\\4\end{array}}{7}$

**7** is the digit of Henry.

**E** is found to vibrate to **5**
**L** is found to vibrate to **3**
**D** is found to vibrate to **4**
**E** is found to vibrate to **5**
**R** is found to vibrate to **9**
$$\overline{26}$$

Add these numbers to find the digit of Elder , $\dfrac{\begin{array}{r}2\\6\end{array}}{8}$

**8** is the digit of Elder. **7 + 8 = 15**
Add to find the digit of the full name **1 + 5 = 6**

**6** is the name vibration of Henry Elder.
He was born January 17, 1872.
January is month **1**.
Day 17; digit of day is **8**.

The year = **1 + 8 + 7 + 2 = 18, = 9**.

Add together month, day and year to find his birth number and we have **1 + 8 + 9 = 18 = 9**.

We find the name vibration of Henry Elder is **6** and his keynote or birth vibration is 9. By the foregoing table of values taken from Balliett's "*Success Through Vibration*" we find his birth vibration is higher than his name vibration, which shows he came to earth this time to work and win in the higher walks of life. His life may be full of failures, but the may be gaining strength through these very failures. From this same key in the same manner as you found the name and birth vibrations of Henry Elder, find every thing in the seen and unseen world.

The numbers vibrate in value as follows:

```
         11
     1   22   9
  2             8
     3       7
        4  6
         5
```

The first three numbers 1, 2, 3, compose the sacred cycle of creation, assimilation and expression. They also denote the action of the mind found in impression, re-impression and expression. When this trinity of numbers is found in digit or single name or birth vibration it shows the power of harmonious expression.

The cube is formed of the numbers **4, 5, 6, 7.** These are the vibrations that seem limited in action, and yet each contains enough success for the happiness of any one bearing it if he seeks the highest of his vibrations.

The unlimited numbers of freedom are **8, 9, 11**; to these is added **22**, which is closely related to **11**.

Pythagoras considers **1** and **22** as numbers possessing a mystical character, as they are the beginning and the end of the Hebrew alphabet. **11** begin the highest point of its vibration and **22** possesses the character of **2** with added strength and freedom.

Find musical key by birth vibration.

| c | d | e | f | g | a | b |
|---|---|---|---|---|---|---|
| **1** | **2** | **3** | **4** | **5** | **6** | **7** |
| **8** | **9** | | | | | |

**22** expresses the full octave of d
**11** expresses the full octave of c

## CHAPTER 3

# If We Have Individual Colors, When and How Did We First Receive Them?

We all feel that certain colors exert more influence over us than others. For days and weeks we may hold to one color and then suddenly tire of it. Sometimes we do not seem to seek another–it seeks us. There is cause for this as there is for a piece of furniture appearing harmonious in one room and inharmonious in another. A rug and a wall paper have different characters in different rooms.

A fruit may be greatly appreciated one season and the following year we may be indifferent to it, only after other seasons have come and gone to find our former taste restored. Friends often share the same fate; not that love is dead, because it will be again renewed.

To get a scientific cause for these expressions of life, to understand what has been taught us by Pythagoras, Plato, Aristotle and Socrates, we must realize that these philosophers were mystics. A mystic at that time, as at the present, believed in the Oneness of All; that everything came from one source; that every separate thing was entirely dependent upon every other separate thing, and yet all the separate things were joined in the Great Universal Chain of Infinite Lives.

We have had many beautiful theories of colors and of the auras which surround us, called also astral colors which are controlled by our birth months, but no one has yet been able to tell us how these months came by their colors. I have explained my theory before many scientific men and women and asked them to correct any statement I made which was not true. I now ask you to do the same, as I am ready to accept a better theory should one offer.

This is the way in which I believe we receive our colors. Mineralogists teach that storms are caused by different planets which approach each other in high heaven. Some are classed as friendly, others as malevolent, and still others as neutral. Each planet is loaded with its own kind of minerals and is revolving at its own rate of vibration. Nature in all parts shows a three-fold motion–the trinity of three parts made one is expressed in every seed, in every bud and in man. So each mineral in a planet has its coarse, fine and finer part. For instance take copper. Its finer part is verdigris, which forms upon the surface when exposed to the air. This makes the astral color of the mineral copper and is called the mystical part. But it is not mystical, it is real.

Iron throws out the red found in iron rust. In coal we find the iridescent colors of the prism. These colors belong to these especial minerals, each mineral having its own color. When a planet approaches another the mineral that predominates in that world is sending out its colors filling full the surrounding atmosphere with its tint.

If the planet it has approached has harmonious coloring, it is considered a friendly planet. When they are not harmonious, the storms that are caused mean no more than do the stinging words between people who love each other. They are simply a conflict of cosmic color.

The first breath the child breathes into its little body in the objective world is the breath that is filled with the color of the atmosphere; it absorbs its rays and branches from center to circumference, from circumference to center. The thousands of individual cells in its body take up this breath and claim it as its own. The purity of the color depends upon the spiritual development of the individual. One artist will reach heights of color another beside him will never realize. So in men and women, it is not so much the color as the power back of the color.

When a soul is born into the world it has almost the strength of the grown man or woman, but it is badly equipped to express itself in earth life. It must conform to nature's laws and develop a fit body to do its work in an active world. The helplessness of the child's weak body is a type of our own relation to our higher self.

The strength of the parent no doubt has some effect on the child's desire to be born at a certain time. But we must not forget that the child is often stronger than its parents.

A man can run an engine when it is properly adjusted, with fire and coal and water, but it is necessary to have power back of the engine to make it move. The spirit force started the lungs before they could begin to act. So two persons may be born at the same instant and each will select or attract of the colors about him the tones he finds himself attuned to. He may select the lifeless tones in any color and live in the vibration to which they respond, or he may see, a low vibration and exalt it until it expresses a great work done in a lonely place.

## CHAPTER 4
## The Use of Birth Vibrations

As colors have different rates of vibration the color or colors of the birth vibration is the most important as it colors all the environment through which you must make the journey of life. When the journey shall be finished all the victories won will be tinged with this color and when the soul comes back for other work the victories gained in the last life will be stored as character and will then be expressed in a name number which vibrates to this color or colors. Individual bodies have certain predominating minerals. A No. 2 has lived or is living in the gold color, as 2 vibrates to gold. An 11 and the other free numbers attract all the colors of the other free numbers. An 8 may not have gained all the vibrations belonging to 9, 11, 22, but it may return to repair weak points of character or as a messenger.

When persons meet as individuals they often clash, as do planets, from the inharmony of their colors. These things are no more than expressions of harmony or inharmony on the physical plane. Developed souls by love become one with all things. Every person, no matter what his condition, vibrates at least one color that is in harmony with every other person and for strength of body and soul that vibration should be recognized.

The fullness of life is measured by the number of vibrations one gives and receives. Keep the palette clean with love and no impure color will remain upon it.

The name is the force and color of the aura of the individual; the birth vibration is the color through which you chose to pass this incarnation. When the colors about you seem dark and unwholesome, go to the centre of light within–ask reverently may flow out through every cell of your body and watch it go happily forth changing gloom to joy.

If you live at your highest all things are friends, no matter how they appear. Nothing good or evil can approach you or enter into your body or environment that has not been attracted by yourself, by some thought or deed of the past. Everything in the Universe is trying to adjust itself to highest good. Every act of faith and thought of kindness helps in the cosmic adjustment of the race. The highest ideal for man is the Christ. The man who strives to lead the Christ life approaches the ideal man. People may try to crucify him, but if he holds to the Christ who overcame death, the cross and the turmoil will dissolve in peace. The aura of the force of his nature, which expresses itself in the color of his name, can be made strong and pure and no harm can penetrate it from without. Nothing but a vibration from within the man's own mind can harm him.

The color of the birth vibration must ever be kept before the mind and eye, as these colors grow dull and impure when the thoughts are impure, but down to their deepest shades become bright and radiant as the result of true thinking.

**Pythagoras of Samos**
(ca. 560-ca. 480 BC)

*Pythagoras was an Ionian Greek philosopher often revered as a great mathematician, mystic and scientist.*

*He believed that everything could be reduced to numbers: the whole universe had been built using mathematics. They said the truth behind the everyday reality we experience lies in numbers.*

*Modern physicists are on a quest to find the equations that prove the 'theory of everything' or the 'grand unification' are Pythagoreans.*

*Pythagoras believed that the planets produced sounds while tracing out their orbits, producing the "harmony of spheres," among many other interesting ideas.*

## CHAPTER 5

## The Meaning of Colors as Disclosed Through Vibrations of Numbers as Taught by Pythagoras

Pythagoras taught that the world and the Heavens and all therein vibrate to the digits, which means any number from 1 to 9.

If we have colors we must have rates of vibration, and if we vibrate we must vibrate at our own rate and consequently each must also have its own sound. The law of Rhythm is founded upon Nature's scientific laws and all things are vibrating in rhythm. And so the month and its day, and the year of your birth give the colors and note, called the key-note you are expressing in life. The key-note of life allows the soul to make the body an open door for the Triune God to use. No vibration should be closed that leads to anything in Earth, Air, Fire and Water. We should eat and drink the same food our fellow men use–this is one way to comprehend Divine and Human fellowship leading to a knowledge of the Universal Brotherhood.

Christ gave us a glimpse of what the body should be when he dropped the coarser particles and appeared in one so fine it was no longer in bondage to physical laws. If you spell out the vibration of Christ it is 5. 5 is also pink, the color of the white light with a touch of flesh.

Christians say Jesus was born on December 25. The digit of the 12th month is 3, of the 25th day is 7. 7 and 3 make 10 or 1. Flame is the color of 1.

1 is a principle and belongs to all persons. Anyone who has come to a consciousness of the Divine and Human Oneness has been born with the flames of the Christ principle and is a light bearer.

1 vibrates flame, 2 gold, 3 should express 1 and 2, making a gold flame.

**B** vibrates to **2**
**L** vibrates to **3**
**U** vibrates to **3**
**E** vibrates to **5**
$$\overline{13 = 4}$$

4 is the vibration of Blue.

**G** vibrates to **7**
**R** vibrates to **9**
**E** vibrates to **5**
**E** vibrates to **5**
**N** vibrates to **5**
$$\overline{31 = 4}$$

4 is the vibration of Green.

**P** vibrates to **7**
**I** vibrates to **9**
**N** vibrates to **5**
**K** vibrates to **2**
$$\overline{23 = 5}$$

5 is the vibration of Pink.

**O** vibrates to **6**
**R** vibrates to **9**
**A** vibrates to **1**
**N** vibrates to **5**
**G** vibrates to **7**
**E** vibrates to **5**
$$\overline{33 = 6}$$

6 is the vibration of Orange, also of Scarlet and Heliotrope found in the same way.

**S** vibrates to **1**
**T** vibrates to **2**
**E** vibrates to **5**
**E** vibrates to **5**
**L** vibrates to **2**
$$\overline{16 = 7}$$

7 is the vibration of Steel, Purple, also of Brick and Magenta found in the same way.

C vibrates to 3
A vibrates to 1
N vibrates to 5
A vibrates to 1
R vibrates to 9
Y vibrates to 7
$$26 = 8$$

8 is the vibration of Canary.

R vibrates to 9
E vibrates to 5
D vibrates to 4
$$18 = 9$$

9 is the vibration of Red.

C vibrates to 3
R vibrates to 9
E vibrates to 5
A vibrates to 1
M vibrates to 4
$$22$$

22 is the vibration of Green.

**W** vibrates to **5**
**H** vibrates to **8**
**I** vibrates to **9**
**T** vibrates to **2**
**E** vibrates to **5**
$$\overline{29 = 11}$$

11 is the vibration of White, Black, Yellow and Violet.

All the other colors can be found in the same manner.

## CHAPTER 6

# Exercises to Develop Your Own Vibration or Birth Digit–The First Trinity

### No. 1

If your name number or birth digit as a whole is 1, place one foot directly in front of the other at a distance of 12 inches–raise right arm perfectly straight in front of ear, the first finger pointing upward, left arm straight at side with finger pointing downward. Think of yourself as a line of strength and truth made by the creator when the world was formed. This line stands today as the principle of life and expresses the Unity of all things. You should be able to help those who wish to understand this unity. If you do not understand this principle and break or disrupt it in your own mind your weakness lies right here. Your force is broken. To understand it, stand as this line shows, with one hand pointing to the highest, the other in the earth vibrations. Breathe slowly as though bringing it through feet, legs, and up through the body following the line through bowels, stomach and vocal organs through the face to the top of the head. Expel slowly, sending the current down back of head, through back of neck, pausing at back of neck, and solar plexus, down through the vertebrae using each section as a step until the base is reached. Now pause and realize it at this point as well as in the solar plexus lying back of the stomach and at the base of the brain that the reservoirs lie, in which magnetism is stored. Send the current to earth the same as when inhaling. Repeat five times. Do this daily, changing position of feet and hands from right to left. Breathe without allowing a break in the current at any place in the body. It is unity you wish to express and if the vibration breaks, stop and try again until you succeed. Then stop for that time. If the current is sent from head to foot unbroken, it is life-giving. But if the law is broken, inharmony, upon all planes is the result. Hum the note of C.

## No. 2

If you are No. 2 you will find yourself benefitted by this exercise:

Stand with arms outstretched directly in front of ear, with the shoulders, hands and fingers in a straight line.

Stand on the balls of both feet, placed parallel. Draw slowly a breath from the depths of earth as a vehicle for the force. Bring it slowly through the body up to the head and let it pass out through your arms and fingers in straight lines, also sending out a vibration from the top of the head, withdraw the lines, making them return with an incoming breath from fingertips and top of head, sending it slowly down through your body to the earth. Do this and you will see the lines come and go outside of your body. They are your own vibrations controlled by concentration and have in them the magnetic force that opens doors you long to open in the spiritual and material world. 2 in Geometry is lines. You stand for it, one line Spirit, the other Matter. When Spirit rules it governs matter; when Matter is allowed to rule, the man weakens in spiritual strength.

When expelling breath, hum the note B–let it pour through your arms and out at the top of your head–send it out in straight lines, and make it return and pass down into the earth. Let the strength come from the diaphragm, forcing the sound B tone through the solar plexus, out in two straight lines as far as possible, pressing it out without limit of distance.

## No. 3

If your name digit or birth vibration is 3, to be a perfect character you must express the two preceding vibrations, 1 and 2.

The 2 character is a combination of 1 and its own. You are to express them both.

Remember always that you are emotional and impressionable, and unless you keep your own high ideals always present, you are liable to be swayed by your surroundings and to express anything offered to you for expression. You must be so firmly rooted and grounded in truth that it will be impossible for anything below your ideals to find a channel of expression through you.

Your vibration is the Christ number for the uplifting of the race–it is through the 3, 6, and 9 expression is given. If this principle were kept clearly in mind, music, literature and all the arts would be uplifted and the eduction of the race would make rapid progress. You are the 3 principle, the Trinity, which is found in all nature–in Father, Son and Holy Spirit, in Body, Soul and Spirit, in Father, Mother, Child. In nature Unity in Diversity Makes Harmony. Your note is E; hum and sing it and use the 1 and 2 exercises, but with them use your own especial note.

The first three numbers, 1, 2, 3, compose the first Trinity. 1, of course, is C, 2 vibrates D and 3 vibrates E. Now 3 may join with the C of 1 and make a perfect harmony, or it may make an incomplete harmony by expressing only the D of the 2. Virtually C, D, E all belong to 3, and it rests with each individual 3 to say what notes or harmony it will express.

Your success depends upon always keeping yourself intact, expressing the trinity of Father, Son and Spirit. Every joy and pleasure ever expressed in the world is contained in this trinity of 3. If there is a sting beneath a pleasure that pleasure is not in the right vibration for you; look a little higher and you will find its counterpart there with a lasting joy the other did not know. When you do this the higher seems to weary the lower and finally drives it out of your environment.

## No. 4

If your name digit is 4 or your birth vibration is this active number, stand on the balls of both feet–place your hands on your hips, elbows straight out shoulder well back– draw your breath up through your legs and pass it would through our elbows. Send it out until you can feel the force leave you like streams of blue light. Keep your chest raised and abdomen well drawn back. Do this five times, then straighten the arms at the sides from the shoulders, clinch the fist and send the force with the breath out through the arms and head; walk four steps with energized legs, holding breath well energized, then relax. Do this four times and hum not note of F with these exercises.

## No. 5

If 5 is the digit of your name or birth vibration, stand erect and draw a long breath, bringing the force from the earth up through your feet and legs, raise the arms even with the shoulders in all directions, front, sides, with one in front and one in back; hold perfectly still and send the breath out in all directions from the finger tips of the open hands. Hum or sing the note of G; then send the breath out strongly energized through the eyes until they seem like burning streams of force. Do not open them unduly wide, but make them channels for the vibration; let the force come from the solar plexus and feel the inflowing and outflowing vibrations at the same time. Concentrate your thoughts on this exercise and exclude everything else from your mind. When you can do this, it will show the kind of growth a 5 needs to make.

## No. 6

If the digit of your name or birth vibration is 6, know the desirable thing for you to gain is rest in motion–complete rest and complete motion. This is Pythagoras' Law of Opposites. When labor of any kind is found beneath your hand, do it actively with an inner feeling of repose. The law of cheerfulness lies unobserved in this triple union of the odd and even 2 and the energetic 4 with its vivid interest in all living things from the insect of the hive all the way up to man. It is the highest working number. It should endeavor to demonstrate the union of Spirit with the internal currents, holding the internal to the external until they culminate in the freed vibration of 8.

You should be a home of rest to those in your environment and the same people can be thrown by you into a tumult. Only by the action of the Spirit can the still small voice be found.

Your exercise is clear only to yourself and from it you can gain the most perfect idea of your place in the universe when raised to your proper spiritual height, where within your activity is found the rest which is its pivotal point.

Reach out your arms and hold them high in the upper air–twin should are they of rest and motion–lay one over the other and hold them so until you feel the circulation of the body equalized, then force all your strength into the hands held tight over your head. Fold one over the other and sing in a clear voice the song of your life– found in the way your name is delineated to you. Hold your hands in this position until the last notes are sung, then say "Father, Son and Holy Spirit, lead my soul into the Divine light of the blessed trinity." Fold your hands again and again as though in submission. Then let your thoughts turn to the things of the outer world filled with universal love and hold this thought of love for all things until you feel you have strength to meet equally the cares and burdens of the world.

## No. 7

If your name digit or birth vibration is 7, stand or sit with body passive; if sitting, with hands lying in lap and hold the thought of the source of all life flowing into the innermost recesses of your being, where is stored the knowledge of Spirit and Matter. In this reservoir is stored the force ready and waiting to aid both you and every other soul incarnate. You cannot advance alone. Your gifts gained by selfishness will drop from you, for they have never been bathed in the pure waters of life.

Every day, sitting, standing, or lying, hold to the strength at the centre, call it diaphragm or solar plexus, it matters not, and breathe a deep breath as coming through all parts of your body to this one centre. Then holding firmly to this one point send out streams of love until there is not an atom in your body that does not vibrate to this good thought. Send it afar to everyone who needs it. It holds in latency just the thing suffering souls need and you clear their atmosphere and make it possible for them to get what they need for their highest good. Send this vibration to those whom you do not love as well as to those whom you do love. You will soon find yourself freed from the bondage of resentment.

As you push out this vibration, sometimes sing the note of your birth, which is B–or fa–sing it out clearly and hum it until you feel it vibrate through and through your body and clear your brain of mental images of past impressions. Hold most firmly to the digit of birth in these exercises, but combine with it the digit of each name you bear and strike each one clearly and the digit of the whole.

You wish to feel the birth vibration most strongly because that vibration contains the experiences you long to meet and store with the character vibrations you have already gained in the great life struggle. 7 is the number that holds all the notes of the musical gamut of sound. It is the physical expression of the universal language called music. It is the musical instrument that the universal notes can be made upon. It can as well be used to express noise as to express harmony. A musical note is universal because it has fulfilled the law of harmony as has 11, 22.

A note holds within itself what the 7 holds and cannot express. As 7 is not free, it holds and feels the perfect power it cannot liberate, especially when the birth number is 7, unless it has with it a free number. 7 holds the melody of the universal within its grasp and seeks to free it.

## CHAPTER 7

## Exercises
*(Continued)*

## Free Numbers

### No. 8

If your name or birth number is 8, your soul knows freedom and with many stripes has tried to make your brain realize it. You should stand ready to help every other should sing his own song of life. Your higher self longs to pick up the discarded notes of your fellow man, be he prince or peasant, for the soul knows no difference, and to help him find the beauty of his own life song.

You have reached the foreground of expression and all notes are in your soul only waiting there for you to give them expression in the world they desire to bring into harmony.

Your greatest power lies in the sound of C. Strike it clearly in all its ranges and hum it sending its vibration to every part of your body and brain. Sing also the combination of your birth, the digit notes of month, day and year, finishing with the digit of the whole, striking it with precision. Also use the exercises of 1, 2, 4, 6, using your own life sounds.

## No. 9

If 9 is the digit of your name or birth vibration, the almost whole gamut of sound is yours. If you have not brought from the depths of your own nature the wealth of treasure that lies there, you have lost the supreme joy of living and have been punished with many trials.

You should realize by this time that all souls are as one soul and that your soul and the Great Soul know no difference between them. They are in constant communion and only the cloak of flesh holds them apart. To stand apart, separating yourself by discordant vibrations is a false position for you as a 9 to hold. You no longer are the expression of a separate soul, but represent the great free body of universal Brotherhood and yet you may be expressing the exact opposite and acting as a discordant in the choir of the music of the Spheres.

You should help every brother who is striving to make the vibration you now hold. He may outrun you in the race for the perfect life we are still striving for, the life showing in the vibrations of 8, 9, 11, 22 when they are not won as a whole. The master is trying to use you for the betterment of the race. The note for your individual development is D. Sing it as your chief helper if it is your birth vibration and use any or all of the exercises of 1, 3, 5, and 7. Using their vibration or Spirit note recall their memories, and if you hold to their highest, you will find in them latent aid. Remember, you are your brother's keeper and without outward demonstration or desire for worldly gain pick up their notes when they falter, and your own song will be enriched as you help others.

## No. 22

If 22 is the digit of your name or birth vibration, you reached the consolidation of human song. You are the avowed burden bearer for souls who need your aid. Your soul is not waiting for them to break the harmony, but when they falter in their life song you unconsciously join in with them until from your strong vibration they grow brave and resume with joy the journey of life.

You must sing with others or your own song will be weakened and enemies instead of friends will confront you.

Your own especial notes are found in the octave of D struck together–the highest and the lowest. Never look for others to aid you. The Father leads you, and yours is not the path of poverty. You have stored wealth in the past. You have had it and been a good steward or you would not be a 22. Vex not yourself as to your path in life–it is God's life and God's path. Simply trust and do your best and you cannot be overthrown or feel the pangs of poverty. You are the accepted child of the Spirit. All the exercises and breaths in the whole gamut of vibration are yours.

## No. 11

If 11 is the digit of your name or birth number the octave of C is calling you. In your own notes is found the foundation of all music and you are one of the leaders in the world's great chorus. And yet it is possible that this soul of yours is shut up in a body that encloses it like a coat of mail. If so, it is possible that you swear like a fiend at the struggles and groans of this angel self striving for release. It is no wonder the angels weep to see men, who have been God's helpers on the silent side of life, so fallen from their high estate in the visible world.

But an 11, 22, 9, or 8 can easily turn and bring their objective and subjective parts in harmony.

All the exercises and breaths in the whole gamut of vibrations are yours. You have made a great victory. Do not soil your beautiful soul life with one false note. You are God's messenger to help humanity in every way and place and the songs all they are singing are also your songs.

## CHAPTER 8
## Your Name–Its Color and Sound

You will often hear it said, "My name is an accident–that which my parents just happened to give me." This is never true. You will admit the soul is older than your present lifetime. It takes the value from life to think that God or Nature has supreme favorites, to some of whom He gives all good things while others go destitute. In this there would be no justice. If man's soul has not always lived it must have an end, because that which has a beginning must logically come to an end. The body dies and is cast aside like a worn out garment, but the soul lives on getting experience of all kinds with the single end in view of becoming a perfect character. The ideal must have been implanted in the ray before it left the Godhead. The ideal man is Jesus, who came to show us what a man should be. The man who in any station in life is doing his best, is making strong vibrations which will show as free numbers. Every act done with a lofty aim opens a vibration of the soul, which lets in the natural sun, and the Son of God is born again. Because a man is not holding a high place in the world does not show he is not able to do so. In some past life he may have had honors, wealth and education. When again coming to earth, when his spiritual sight was undimmed, he chose his own time of birth, to secure the vibration he is now filling. He knew to be born of such parents and to live amid such environment was what he needed to enable him to grow into greater manhood.

A man who has been educated in past lives will have wisdom. We often say of such people they do not need teacher and book. They came to improve in humble traits of character, as may be seen by their birth digit, which is usually 4, 5, 6, or 7. Such men may be giants in knowledge but they seldom rise to the great places in the material world. If they live at their very highest, success may crown them, but they work for work's sake, and the world is inclined to let them go unrewarded. When such a man has a name with strong vibrations men respect and love him. When a man has an 8, 9, 11, or 22 in his birth path he came for honors and to work in the great places of life; but often those who possess them, and they are of their own choosing, fall into the gamut below.

Your name will show you where your melody lies, also the motive you are using to gain the vibration you desire. You may have in past lives developed the spiritual side of your nature to the exclusion of the physical side and not have fulfilled the complete law of body, soul and spirit. You may have a name like Mary Patterson, Mary 3 and Patterson 11. 3 always stands for expression, so 3, 11 would show she had already expressed the spiritual. This time she may have come with a birth path of 4 and she will be constantly annoyed to find she knows so little of the really practical things of life. She will be likely also to annoy her friends until her vibration becomes attuned to the earth currents.

Another may have expressed the physical side of life with name 4, 5, 4. This man knows the world and humanity, but the highest conception of God is unknown to him. He knows God through man and man's love, but is not attuned to spirit. He will have to seek that which is lacking to make high number vibrations.

## CHAPTER 9
## Reading Individual Name Vibrations– The First Trinity

### No. 1

If your name digit is 1, you stand as a foundation for others to build upon. It is your mission to hold to Unity in all things. Let others falter, but you must remain steadfast.

When you break the Law of Unity and resent the seeming injustices of the world, you close the vibration to human hearts, and also to the peace of the spirit. Your vibration of 1 is a hidden esoteric flame burning the self-hood from your nature. When this shall be accomplished, it will drop into the white ashes of the 11th vibration and rise free into objective as well as subjective life. This will not occur if you break the unity you came to maintain. Should you break this unity, you will suffer periods of disaster, usually occurring every seven years. This number of 1 opens the door to the life of a mystic, as was Socrates, Browning, Emerson and many more of our great inventors and philosophers. It means Unity, the binding together of all things and the understanding of life as whole. When failure of cosmic consciousness is recognized, of all vibrations i is the most miserable. When living with but not under its vibration the flame, which is its color, can be a cloud by day and a pillar of fire by night. You have almost completed the entire cycle at least once, lacking only the 1, which makes the 11. If you fulfill your mission by holding and maintaining unity, you will make the 11th vibration in this life. It is a gold flame.

## No. 2

The color of No. 2 is gold and mineral predominates in the body when a No. 2 is living at his highest. This number has no middle ground; it is either vibrating to 1, spirit or its opposite, matter. When holding to 1 it is musical and brings together the harmonies in earth currents to express music–it is then able to draw from all sources to adjust all currents to harmony. When living in the earth currents, the spiritual vibrations move in a closed body, which expresses weakness and disease. They are attuned to the pipe organ and golden instruments should be used, as this mineral belong to 2.

No. 2 has either very strong muscles or weak ones– there is no middle ground. If the digit of your name is 2, Gold is your color. No especial flower has 2. This does not mean you do not love them, but they have little part in your composition. Your body to all kinds of supersensitive odors. As your bird is a bird of paradise, it is probable you have lived in past incarnations where you have become familiar with them. All things vibrating 1, 2, 3 belong to each other and to you.

If your name vibrates 2, you show you have had the advantage of a classical musical training somewhere in the past and composers of the vibrations of Grieg, Flotow, Boehm, Rubenstein, Puccini and Verdi have been familiar to you. If it is your birth vibration, study these masters.

No. 2 has no relation to fruits.

Your guardian angels are St. John and St. Ursula. The cross is your symbol. The part that points to Heaven is the 1 part, when man's will crosses God's will it becomes a cross. Hold to the first part.

## No. 3

This number is the vehicle of expression. It is the work of 3 to reveal the hidden, to brush from sealed eyes the earth dust so that others may see the glory of the divine all about them. When vibrating in its true key, it is a beautiful, happy number.

It can express a boundless Christ love and, when occasion demands, show to the world the horror of a faithless nation.

As beauty abounds so freely in this world, so we find the 3 a joyous and happy nature. Whenever you find this vibration in a name, it always wishes to express the vibration before or after it. When it is found in the birth number, it means you came to re-express the vibrations found in the name number.

It has no colors of its own, it must express the color of 1 vibration, a gold flame.

This number closes the Trinity and is considered as vibrating at a high commercial rate as seen by the chart, the swing from right to left being a long distance.

Suppose your name is Mary Jones. Mary vibrates 3, Jones 9. The meaning is that Mary has expressed the high free soul nature in the past and now she may come with a No. 4 or No. 6 birth path. She holds latent within her soul these beautiful high vibrations and may not be wholly conscious of them and be living now in a lower birth vibration to gain mastery of a weak point in her soul's growth. It always means expression.

3 closes the first Trinity of Body, Mind and Spirit. 3 expresses this Trinity. The mind works first by impression. You see the words I have written? This is 1. If you let them sink into your mind and then put them together in words, that is re-impression or No. 2. No. 3 is expression. Not to express yourself in some way weakens the individual. The stronger the impression, the clearer the re-impression, the better will be the expression, and it will express either negative or positive conditions. E as well as C and D have much to tell you. Always sing the air or chords that lie under your hand, as it is the mission of 3 to express. If 3 is your name number, you have already

expressed it, then express your birth number.

If the digit of your name is 3, you have been a Peacemaker and you have given freedom to humanity. If your birth number is 3 these are the things of interest to you in life. Your liver, glands and blood are either the strongest or weakest part of your body.

If your name number is 3, you have had amethysts, amber and rubies and should now be strong enough to bring them to you as gifts.

You have been familiar with and known radium. Your flowers show no especial climate, as the rose, orchid, forget-me-not, pansy, nasturtium and wild olive can life in many climates; also your body, to a sensitive nostril, should throw out the odor of rose or dactylis as Plutarch tells of Alexander.

Your birds show grandeur, as the eagle and the swan.

Your past incarnations have been rich in music, as you show familiarity with Schumann, Puccini, Mozart and are related to composers vibrating 1 and 2.

Your trees speak of a southern clime in mahogany and redwood. Your fruits are grapes and lime.

The instrument you have played on is the trombone.

You vibrate to all angels. Mary is your patron saint, and the wreath, which is endless, is the emblem you have expressed.

If your birth vibration is 3, all these things you must seek, buy, or in some way acquire.

3 is a sacred number and is always found closely associated with 7 and 11. 1, 2, 3 are higher in vibration than 4, 5, 6, 7, but not as high as 8, 9, 11, 22.

3 is a principle running though all numbers, and when found in a name shows the owner knows what mental unity means and has attained some time in past lives glimpses of Cosmic Consciousness 8, 9, 11, 22 possesses. The Cosmic Consciousness, which may be illustrated by this story told of a youth who wanted to go into the temple to administer the rites of the order, but the priest thought he had not made the connecting link of consciousness between the human and the divine. So he told the lad to go out into the world and bring back one thousand horses for his God. The lad was without money, but he went out into the streets and began crying "My God wants one thousand horses, my God wants one thousand horses" He went about for days and nights repeating this cry until at last the people wearied of hearing it and finally were touched with compassion and one and another began bringing in a horse. The cry went on and the horses increased in number until men volunteered to care for them. By this time the boy was crying nothing but "God–horses," and finally, utterly unmindful of the result of his words, the boy merely whispered "God."

He took the horses to the priest as a gift from God and man. The unity had been made by a thousand persons and the priest took the lad into the temple as one who had gained Universal Consciousness.

So persons vibrating to the high numbers, 8, 9, 11, 22 have in some past life done something that opened to them cosmic intelligence. Persons who have not a strong number may make one in this life by holding fast to one high unselfish principle until it sinks into the body vibration.

It is a grave mistake to think a word cannot be made to reach far out and far into the spiritual world. Your thought, when using a word, tones its vibration. Take the word God. This expression of the Divine has the 8th free vibration. The word Divine has the free 9th–Jesus is 11–Christ vibrates to 5. This number, according to Pythagoras, stands for masculine and feminine. After Christ arose he possessed this quality. When we mention or think of a name, it starts that person's vibration and instantly attacks others in the same vibration. The feeling is according to the thought. So in this way, a strong vibration opens the way for intercourse with strong people. The same is true of the weak vibrations.

## CHAPTER 10
## Reading Individual Name Numbers—
## 4, 5, 6 7

### No. 4

If your name digit is 4, you have passed in safety the F note and know the secrets of that musical vibration. What you now desire to do lies in the note of your birth path. If 4 is your birth number, find all there is in 4 or F. Of all the numbers this is the most personal; it deals with intellect and judges everything both in the seen and unseen world from an intellectual standpoint. If you live in the highest part of your vibration, you will build, by your own energy, landmarks along life's pathway on which your name will be carved; if you drop to the vibration of self, ignoring your fellow workers, your monuments will crumble and another builder, working with higher motives, will take your place. It is your patriotic duty to protect your family and country. It is in your vibration to do it, and if you have not sufficient bodily vigor to do it, you are not living in your own vibration. No. 4 means physical and mental strength.

Green and blue vibrations have surrounded you from your first breath. These are the colors of the earth and sky, a green earth to live upon and a blue sky that tells you that just above the intellect there is a plane of spirit that will open to you when intellect can go no further and your highest self claims the wisdom that lies there ready when you shall have grown into a knowledge of its presence. This is the work found in the blue vibration. The green shows you the green foliage of earth and the banks of commerce. To own land and to appropriate it for self and family is the desire of a person working in the 4 vibration. If you have passed the 4, as show by having it in your name, do not let your past propensities govern you. The birth vibration is the one in which to gain the things you came to seek.

Your larynx is either your strongest or weakest part. When living in harmony, the voice of No. 4 is capable of a sweetness unknown to other vibrations. When disgruntled, it is most unpleasant.

Your gems are the emerald and bloodstone; the green stone speaks for the earth's harmony, the red for the brotherhood of all humanity, which is a difficult thing for a 4 to grasp. It is its esoteric message.

Your minerals, those that predominate in your body, if your name is 4, are coal, ochre and silver.

You understand what coal does? It is one of the world's principal motive powers and supplies heat and light to homes. This is your kind of work. You will work for silver dollars and should use silver articles as much as you desire–the metal belongs to you.

Your flower is the fuchsia. This fragile flower has a lesson for you.

Your odor is patchouli.

Your birds are robin, blue-jay and kildeer. These are hardy, self-reliant travelers.

Your higher self is in sympathy with the music of Wagner and Mascagni.

Your trees are hemlock and coffee. The study of these trees will help you to understand the vibrations of your own body.

Your fruits are strawberry and pineapple.

Your vibration shows no musical instrument except the guitar.

Your patron saint is St. Luke.

One of your symbols is a star.

A person working in the 4 vibration (birth number), comes to work and gains intellectual knowledge. He should graduate from all the schools and colleges possible. When he passes on, in later incarnations, he will carry with him this knowledge and it will appear as wisdom. After a soul has once received a thorough intellectual training, it is seldom born again under circumstances where this can be repeated. It does not need it; it has had it and now another quality needs attention.

If necessary environment to progress were not selected by the Spirit, the soul when blinded by earth dust, might waste precious time.

## No. 5

If your name digit is 5, you have passed that vibration and have stored up knowledge as material to draw upon. If your birth vibration is 5, you are seeking the knowledge contained in it. If you have passed, you have stored away knowledge of the G note and are ready to begin upon the gamut of sound just above the lower octave. Your note is bold, daring, so is your life filled with bold events of short duration. Your wheel of life turns so rapidly in its cycle, you are often forced to wonder what the next event will be. The reason for this is, you have passed the intellectual plane of 4 and stand upon the threshold of the realm of spirit. The tense grip upon material things has been relaxed, and glimpses of the pink light, which is your color, flash upon you, while like a happy child you look out upon the new scene of life.

Your mind wanders in many directions, gathering from every source that which entertains and instructs. The glimpse of the unseen, just beyond, fills you with longings. Sometimes you become so determined to enter this realm, that you force your entrance by will power and become involved in all the horrors of Black Magic.

If you live at your highest, you will generally know the thoughts of others, but do not try to enter the Holy of Holies of another soul. Of all vibrations yours is the most charming and fascinating. It is so adaptable. When an unpleasantness arises, No. 5 seldom injures or hates, but simply turns thoughts in other directions. Many marriages are liable to happen. Money comes and goes. As the fast revolving wheel turns in its course, the pink light may be obscured and another experience will offer. If you are living in your vibration you will accept experience. If you are living along and are having a monotonous life, you are losing the lessons of this spa of life.

To concentrate, to go often into the silence, is the safe-guard of your vibration.

Your mineral is clay–it take many forms and is not injured by use.

Your flowers are the sweet smelling carnation and sweet-peas, and they are like the fascinating 5 character.

Your birds are the cuckoo and flamingo. Study

their character and the study will reveal to you much of yourself.

Your composer is Liszt.

Your fruits are cherry, lemon, cranberry and apple.

Your instruments are the trumpet and the viola.

Your patron saint is St. Gregory.

One of your symbols is the triangle.

## No. 6

If your name digit is 6, you may have passed the 4 and 5 vibrations and thereby gathered the experience needful for your development at that time. But this does not mean that you have necessarily assimilated all the wisdom found in these vibrations.

If your name is Emma, or any other name which vibrates 5, you will know you have made the development of that vibration, but if your name as a whole shows the digit of 6, you will meet the events of life as a 6, when an emergency arises, even if you have a name like William Barlett, of which William vibrates 7 and Bartless 8, each name vibrating higher than you do as a whole. You will in this case, no doubt, get the whole strength of his lower vibration, which will enable you to accomplish work you could not do in any other vibration. Your soul has grown in this manner, showing its own eternal wisdom.

6 is attuned to A. If your name digit is 6 you know the meaning of the A note. If 6 is your birth digit, strike this note upon a well tuned instrument until you can use it correctly with the voice, and listen for the return message. *See it* in company with your colors, orange, scarlet and heliotrope. If 6 is your birth digit, they are the colors that welcomed you to earth; if 6 is your name number, they are friends of the past and their memory lingers in every part of your nature.

In the orange vibration you find power, strength and adaptation to earth life. The reds are limited to scarlet, which is bright and shows how strongly a 6 can feel. Heliotrope is the color of the highest parenthood and the purest love for children. It has a psychic foresight, and when this color is held to, servile work of family cares are lightened.

You should never labor as does one who is working in the 4 vibration. You represent the Saturday of the world's days when the work is almost finished. You should fit everything in its place and do so joyously. When you fail to find joy in your work, it would be better to stop working, until in the silence you have once more found your soul's self, in whom all joy abounds. If you are living in the 6th vibration, any work you may do, in any vocation in life, will be a failure unless it is done with cheerfulness. Those living in the 4 vibration may make the air blue with discord and succeed after a fashion, but it is not so with you.

You should always be dressed with care and precision; be fond of dainty effects and colors; lifting your especial colors of orange, scarlet and heliotrope into their lighter shades, yet always keeping their true tones.

You should know coming events before they reach you, and prepare calmly for their coming, always remembering that what appear as enemies may be friends in disguise. If you cannot do all this, some channel of your vibration is closed, and your lifework and your enjoyment in it are thereby limited. You should not seek to penetrate the future, for your life-work lies in doing the work under your hand.

The strongest and weakest parts of your body are your kidneys, arms, cells, and veins.

Your gems are topaz, diamond, onyx and jasper. If your name digit is 6, you should be strong enough to draw them to you; if your birth digit is 6, you should purchase them.

Your minerals are borax and marble.

Your flowers are tube-rose, laurel and chrysanthemum.

Your odor is japonica.

Your birds are the bunting, gold-finch and falcon.

The composer whose music has a message for you is Schubert. You may remember that his music, before he received any musical education, was superior to other masters under like conditions.

Beethoven also belongs to your vibration.

Your fruits are the orange, quince and mulberry.

The musical instruments you have used, if your name number is 6, and should now study if your birth vibration is 6, is the lyre.

Your guardian angel is Michael, meaning "Who is like God."

Your patron saint is St. Denis.

One of your symbols is the crescent, an emblem of the new life.

## No. 7

If your name digit is 7 and you have a higher vibration in individual parts of your name, as an 8 or 22, you have evidently come to finish work that to your higher self seemed unsatisfactory. If there is no 11 or 22 in your name vibration, you are now ready to enter the higher gamut of free vibration.

You are in the 7 period of rest and reflection and will ever be a mystery to those with whom you come in close contact. They will never understand that you open only the channel it is necessary for you to learn from or to receive into, and it is always solely from your own volition that any channel is opened.

When you wish, you can pour out treasures more lavishly than any other vibration, but when the end is served, you put on the seal again, and no power can force you again to open yourself. Your Sunday has come.

You will always be able to do any kind of work set before you and to do it in a finished manner.

You possess a Sunday air, and should always be dressed daintily, as one is when going to the little chapel with stained glass windows, which keep out the bright sunlight from the altar.

You are refined and bear always an air of elegance, if you are living in your own vibration.

You should always be competent to do tasks not requiring too much grasp, as 7 is not entirely free from the limited gamut of vibrations. Yet should your highest number be a 7, it will be sufficient to enable you to meet every task brought before you by your higher self.

You can do the best work for yourself and others in an individual way, as it is hard for one living in your vibration to give satisfaction to a partner, for the reasons already given.

You are a finisher of all kinds and in this will succeed. Finish everything that presents itself to your own satisfaction and it will be well done as you critical and possess the inner quietness of the Sabbath day.

When you live for self and disregard a Higher Self, the opposite of all this will occur. A work day of unrest will take possession of you and you will be inclined to babble constantly of trifling things, which condition will destroy both health and happiness. Correct this by throwing all the force of your soul to the aid of your higher self instead of the physical self.

## CHAPTER 11
## Free Numbers
## 8, 9, 11, 22

### No. 8

This number is the beginning of a broader and stronger vibration. The pendulum of life swings with broad, clear sweeps from opposite sides of what men call good and evil. So broad and aggressive is its action that those bearing it are generally strongly felt in a community.

8 stands for body, 9 for soul, and 11 for spirit, making the Divine Trinity. They are called strong numbers because they show characters stored with knowledge who are capable of possessing the Cosmic Consciousness. They are the ones who can look out from the strength within themselves and realize the unity of life. They can feel the spiritual kinship of all things from the mineral up through each link in life's chain until they claim the character of the Nazarine.

If the digit of your name is 8, you have received as a reward for faithfulness in the past the power to open the vibration of Cosmic Consciousness. This means freedom; it means that you have glimpses, in an emergency, of the things needed for yourself and others. It is a slight turning away of the mist which makes you see through a glass darkly, and behind it lies the wealth of the Universe.

You can always have this power when your desire is unselfish, for an 8 is his brother's keeper, and to succeed you must know how to live in this vibration so as to seek for others all the blessings you seek for yourself.

When you realize that this has already been gained in the past and that you can again bring it into activity, a great victory will have been gained. It is like drawing a check on your bank of freedom. When you do not live in this way your bondage is pitiable. Your higher self will rack and disturb you until all your surroundings fail to give you pleasure, and the fear of poverty never leaves you. You were intended for an investor, to gain money for others as well as for yourself; to build houses for others under your personal care; to clothe people in such a tactful manner that even the helped forget the clothes came from your bounty.

Look for no return. Work for the race and not for the individual.

It is not easy for those living in limited vibrations to understand this, but you can, if you will look to the higher self, which always longs to aid you and will help you to understand the joy of right living which lies stored in your freed character.

You would be a good corporate lawyer, also a good physician. You should build hospitals and sanitariums and help the inmates to enjoy life.

You should see that your family is properly provided for, as it is the tendency of the world to beg of an 8, something of the same feeling moving with them with which they implore God, which vibrates to 8, something of the same feeling moving with them with which they implore God, which vibrates to 8. People are always saying "Give, give," and then forgetting to give thanks. But you must not expect gratitude and must give even before you are asked.

If you are poor, change your thoughts and methods. Poverty does not belong to you, and only selfishness or a failure to recognize the right can bind you.

Your astral note is high C; from it others build their own melody.

If your name does not vibrate to 8, 9, 11 or 22 and you have a birth path of 8, you will know what the struggle for a life of liberty means. You are a brave soul to work in a stronger vibration than has ever seem strewn with failures, they may not be really failures, but only friends in gloomy dress helping you to make the 8th vibration. This when made (supposing your birth vibration is 8 and you have not a name with a strong number) will so change your character that you will no longer be able to exist under a false vibration and in some way you will change your name. Until this is accomplished you cannot make yourself what you are not. When the world accepts the name with a higher vibration you have earned it. Before you gain it, you will not try to change your name, from a lack of inclination.

Should 8 be your name vibration or one part of your name vibration, the opal is associated with you to that extent and should be recognized. If your birth digit is 8, the gem should be bought and worn; it is a fellow traveler in your journey through life. Should your name digit be 8 or one part of your name, you have somewhere in the past been associated with this gem.

If you live at your highest, those things which have been associated with you in the past, as shown by your name vibration, should come to you by love and without money.

Study the composition of the opal, it will help you to understand the 8 vibration.

## No. 9

If your name vibration is 9, you have made much the same realization of the Cosmic Consciousness related of the 8; but the action is slightly different, as the odd numbers differ somewhat from the even–the odd numbers, as 3, 5, 7, 9 deal more with the realm of mind. The even numbers, 2, 4, 6, and 8, can be divided to form material partnerships and deal more with the bodies of men and their homes.

A 3 always expresses the condition about him; when his environment does not please him he removes himself to a different environment. You as a 9 have latent three times the strength of the 3, and are a power to express good or evil. What appears evil to the world may not appear as evil to you, as you have the wisdom of the cosmic knowing. You hold to what seems to you good, let the world clamour as it will. A 9 makes his own law, as 9 vibrates law.

It would be well for every 9 to go daily to the source of all good and ask help to express only the good.

You are in the vibration of mind; the world is weary of toil and desires pleasure. You are conscious of this desire, and in your strong power you clear the lower vibration, and in so doing temptations of all kinds come to you. They do not originate with you, but belong to the world, and if you allow them to enter your vibration you are liable to catch the spirit of debauch–this is the weakness of your 9th vibration. The strength you came to gain lies in this overcoming. You feel the world is crying for more love; you feel its heart break and can express what it desires. People soon come to feel your sympathy and give you love unstinted. You can hold so much love in your environment that no ill either of the body or spirit can enter there.

A person in a lower vibration may perhaps have the same influence through love that you have, but they gain it by an effort while to you love comes as unconsciously as breath.

A digit of 8,9 , 11, or 22 will show this character, if one of these digits is the full name or one of the names. If they are in the birth vibration, the person is working to gain what you already have stored in your character.

To deal with humanity is the work of all 9s. It means the world's surface and world will be bettered by the projection of yourself when you are living at your highest. You will never be happy until you recognize the Unity of Life and the Universal Brotherhood of Man. You can do this much more easily than a weaker vibration. If you cannot do so, ask your soul to teach you and it will do so from knowledge stored in its own recesses.

You can succeed in expressing or reproducing any work in art or music to which you care to give expression.

You would make a just and humane judge.

Your views are rather broad for an orthodox clergyman, but your congregation would love you and follow your teaching and the dogmas of the church doctrine would be forgotten in the broad faith of God's love.

You would make a dearly loved physician, magnetic and skillful.

You would also succeed as an author of occult works.

Persons bearing an 8, 9, 22, or 11 as digits of names are not confined to single notes in the musical scale–they have, in a degree, conquered them all.

Your individual note, which has been especially conquered, is D. This note, struck or sung, should open up to you the memory of the past. We do not know how far back memory can go, but we do know there are treasures in your being that this note can bring to light. If met, the musical note of your birth vibration will some time show in your character and be added to your name.

If your name digit is higher than your birth digit, you may appear as a dull or commonplace character. This is in consequence of the choice made by your eternal part before you came to earth, in order to give you the experience needed for your soul's true growth. When the earth dust drops from our eyes, we will all know that all vibrations are equally good in God's sight, where high or low, great or small, are qualities unrecognized.

If you have a limited birth vibration, as 4, 5, 6, or 7, do not allow yourself longer to feel their limitation. You have hidden within your being the power to feel the unity of all things the Creator made good. Within you dwell the minerals you vibrate to, all the vegetable world found in your vibration, besides all the insects, etc., which are either your friends or denote some weakness to be overcome.

A 9 vibrates to peacock. This bird covers more of the earth's surface than any other bird. It is an unusual creation; study it well in regard to the law of Opposites–Good or Evil.

If your birth vibration is 9 and your name is not so high, then have patience with yourself while you are earning this much loved free vibration. Study moderation, as in excess lies the pitfall of all high vibrating individuals.

## No. 11

If your name digit is 11, you have made one entire round of the great wheel of life and only the immortal part of you knows the many unsuccessful attempts made before you won this highest vibration, 11. Your memory may run back to the time when you served as a priest in the temple and offered burnt sacrifices for the sins of the world. Today you may be working in another vibration, as shown by your birth path.

If you have not yet made the 11th vibration, but are striving to make it, as shown by your birth path, then know your body is your temple and you wish to vibrate to the Royal Priesthood and to Melchisedek, and you desire to know the laws of the spiritual world as well as you do those of the material world.

If your name digit is 11, within your being is stored the memory of all these truths, and yet today you may be cursing the God whom you have acknowledged as the mighty God of truth. You may be clinging to your family with the tenacity of an animal, when the priest knew nothing beyond the Brotherhood of Man. The priests were supported by the gifts of the people and were not taxed, and yet you may be giving all your attention to material gain. The greatest misers are found among the 11s, when they should take thought of nothing but spiritual truth. If this occurs in one whose birth path is 11, he is losing the value of this incarnation and searing and blackening the soul he loves.

The reason these high vibrations who have made or almost made the entire round sometimes appear as such high-handed sinners, is that when the pendulum of life swings to the extreme of spiritual truth, its return journey is strongest at the opposition of what we call good and evil. These souls may have allowed ambition or spiritual pride to rule them and so have failed to make an 8 or 9 vibration. They may have partly made it, as parts of their name show. These souls will return and return to make the perfect round of life, 8, 9, 11. They appear illy adjusted to life and perplexed by its eternalities. When the journey to the 11th vibration has been made in a harmonious manner, its beauty shows in every act of life. If you have made the 11th and are serving in a lower vibration and are enjoying life, then be sure your past journeys have been profitable in God's sight. It is the ultimate desire of every soul to develop into a perfect Trinity of Body, Soul and Spirit, which growth is shown by an 8, 9, 11, or 22. When these vibrations have been made, God will use you for the interest of the race. As 11 is more spiritual than a 22.

Your musical numbers are the octave of C–all the harmonies found in this octave upon any instrument.

## No. 22

If 22 is the digit of your name, you have reached the 11th vibration by a different route from that followed by the 11th, but the result is much the same. Your journey has been made by the even numbers instead of by the odd, as in 3, 5, 7 and 9.

You understand the physical needs of humanity–homes, hospitals and churches–and you came to finish the temple called the body and to show others the beauty of a perfect temple for the spirit.

When a 22 fails it is usually from love of material gain and not from love of frolic. You have a beautiful, strong vibration; live in its highest part and you will know what the great coordination of the universe means.

Your musical numbers are the octave of D–all the octave notes of D upon any instrument will tell you much of the meeting of spirit and matter; of the parting of the ways which took place in 2, found expression in 3, and its ultimate in 22. In 8 you freed yourself from bondage to the body and in 22 you have grown to behold the vision beyond the intellect.

No one can be a 22 who has not passed through the experiences of 4, 6, 2,8, 9, 1 and probably all the other numbers. But the growth of strength has been made on the even side. When you reached 8 you understood the world in its fullness, but you longed for the love of men as this was beyond you, and so you passed into 9. You then longed for the satisfaction of spirit and may have passed into the 11 and obtained universal knowledge in that way; but more probably you passed directly from 9, to 22 as you now had stored the love of humanity and 22 makes you desire to unite, as does water, the souls and bodies of men.

You who have 8, 9, 22 or 11 in name vibration have stored within your system an understanding of composers. Bizet and Weber vibrate 8; George Frederick Handel, Ponchielli, Gluck and Strauss vibrate 9; Johann Sebastian Bach, Richard Wagner, Saint-Saens and Mendelssohn vibrate 11. All of these composers are in some way related to the spiritual trinity of 8, 9, 22 and 11.

# New Falcon Publications
**Publisher of Controversial Books and CDs**
**Invites You to Visit Our Website:**
**http://www.newfalcon.com**

At the Falcon website you can:

- Browse the online catalog of all our great titles, including books by Robert Anton Wilson, Christopher S. Hyatt, Israel Regardie, Aleister Crowley, Timothy Leary, Osho, Lon Milo DuQuette and many more
- Find out what's available and what's out of stock
- Get special discounts
- Order our titles through our secure online server
- Find products not available anywhere else including:
    - One of a kind and limited availability products
    - Special packages
    - Special pricing
- And much, much more

**Get online today at http://www.newfalcon.com**